SAF

Flashcards

Flashcards for the
SAF Numbering System

Kathy M. Scogna

www.KathyScogna.com

SAF Flashcards

Flashcards for Students of SAF

Thanks to Nic Scogna for his illustration *The Sun*, 1999.

These flashcards are based on the Endocrine Sense Channels Chart, also known as the SAF Operative Chart, as fully explained in *Junk DNA: Unlocking the Hidden Secrets of Your DNA*.

Other Scogna-authored books that define the SAF language (numbering system and words used) are:

The Numbers of SAF—a Client's Handbook

SAF Simplified– Self Awareness Formulas.

Available wherever books are sold or www.KathyScogna.com.

ISBN-13: 978-1516916511 (CreateSpace-Assigned)
ISBN-10: 1516916514

SAF Flashcards

1. SAF 2. SAF Numbers 1-24 3. Energetic healing
I. Kathy M. Scogna, author, editor II Title

Contents

SAF

Flashcards

Flashcards for the
SAF Numbering System

Kathy M. Scogna

www.KathyScogna.com

How to Use this Book to Become Fluent in the Language of SAF!

SAF Flashcards are a quick and easy teaching tool for memorizing the SAF Numbering System.

Each page may be read and memorized in turn, or for use as actual Flashcards for study purposes, these pages may be cut on the dotted lines provided on each page.

Spend as little as 15 minutes per day until you can look at the front (# and Organ title) and recite the Operative words found on the back.

A companion book with details on the numbers and their meanings: *The Numbers of SAF—a Client Guidebook.*

Read also: *Junk DNA: Unlocking the Hidden Secrets of Your DNA*

SAF Simplified: Self Awareness Formulas

Flashcards for the
SAF Numbering System

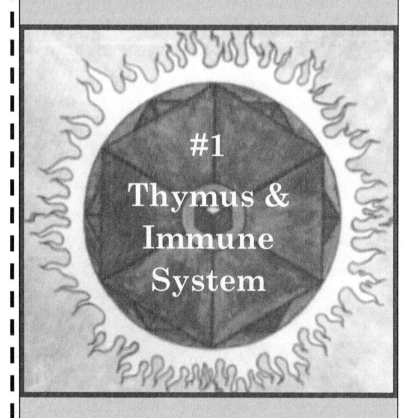

#1
Thymus &
Immune
System

Flashcards for the
SAF Numbering System

#1 Thymus & Immune System

Action: **Against**

Condition: **Protection**

Emotion: **Aggression**

Low Emotion: **Reaction**

High Emotion: **Action**

Flashcards for the
SAF Numbering System

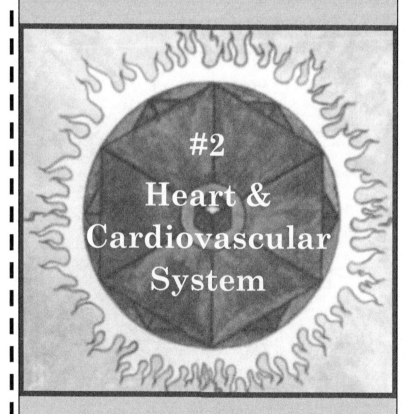

#2

Heart &
Cardiovascular
System

#2 Heart & Cardiovascular System

Action: **Run**

Condition: **Synchronize**

Emotion: **Love**

Low Emotion: **Deny**

High Emotion: **Accept**

Flashcards for the
SAF Numbering System

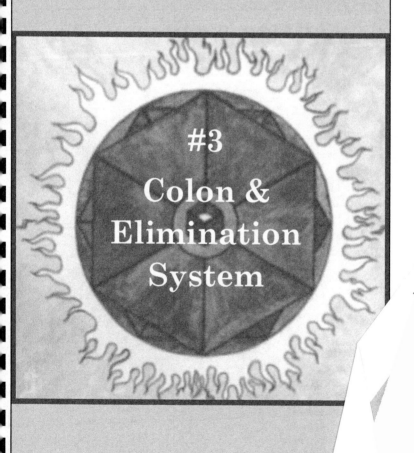

#3
Colon &
Elimination
System

#3 Colon & Elimination System

Action: **Contain**

Condition: **Detoxify**

Emotion: **Hate**

Low Emotion: **Failed**

High Emotion: **Achieve**

Flashcards for the
SAF Numbering System

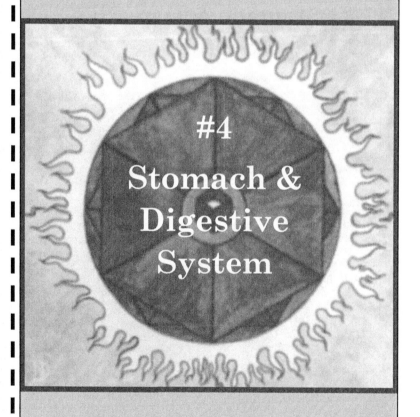

#4

Stomach &
Digestive
System

#4 Stomach & Digestive System

Action: **Dissolve**

Condition: **Digestion**

Emotion: **Happy**

Low Emotion: **Eaten**

High Emotion: **Assimilate**

Flashcards for the
SAF Numbering System

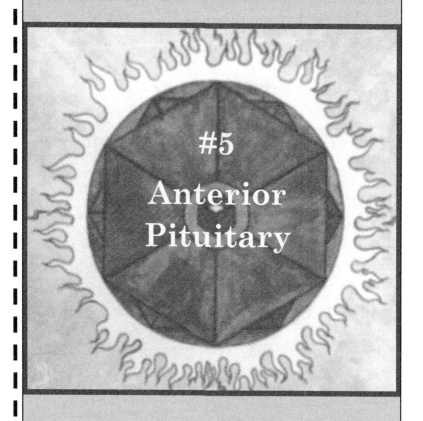

#5

Anterior
Pituitary

#5 Anterior Pituitary

Action: **Direct**

Condition: **Coordinate**

Emotion: **Observant**

Low Emotion: **Controlled**

High Emotion: **Master**

Flashcards for the
SAF Numbering System

#6
Liver &
Gallbladder

#6 Liver & Gallbladder

Action: **Keep**

Condition: **Transmutate**

Emotion: **Sadness**

Low Emotion: **Aged**

High Emotion: **Rejuvenate**

Flashcards for the
SAF Numbering System

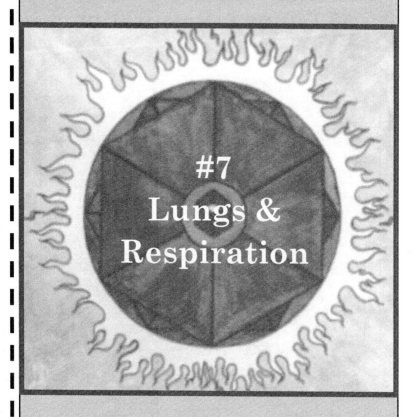

#7
Lungs &
Respiration

#7 Lungs & Respiration

Action: **Exchange**

Condition: **Vaporization**

Emotion: **Monotony**

Low Emotion: **Stifled**

High Emotion: **Refresh**

Flashcards for the
SAF Numbering System

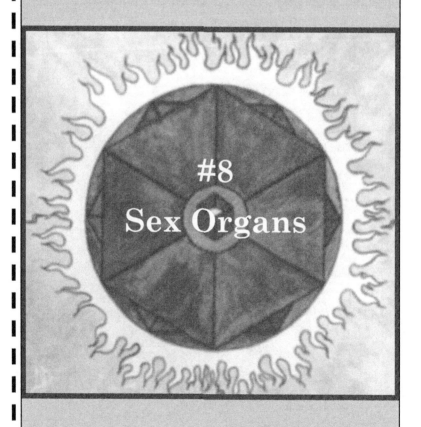

#8
Sex Organs

#8 Sex Organs

Action: **Attract**

Condition: **Reproduce**

Emotion: **Apathy**

Low Emotion: **Separated**

High Emotion: **Create**

Flashcards for the
SAF Numbering System

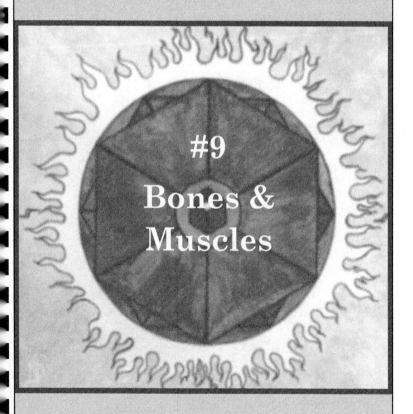

#9

Bones &
Muscles

#9 Bones & Muscles

Action: **Hold**

Condition: **Locomotion**

Emotion: **Pain**

Low Emotion: **Blamed**

High Emotion: **Respond**

Flashcards for the
SAF Numbering System

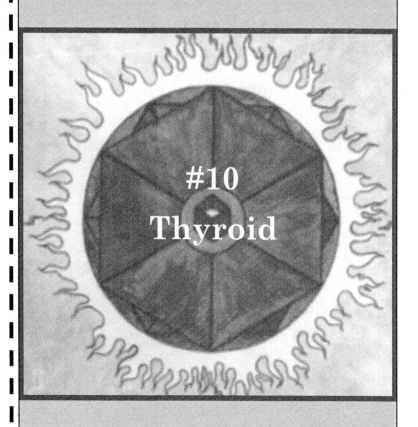

#10
Thyroid

#10 Thyroid

Action: **Action**

Condition: **Metabolization**

Emotion: **Anxiety**

Low Emotion: **Criminal**

High Emotion: **Justice**

Flashcards for the
SAF Numbering System

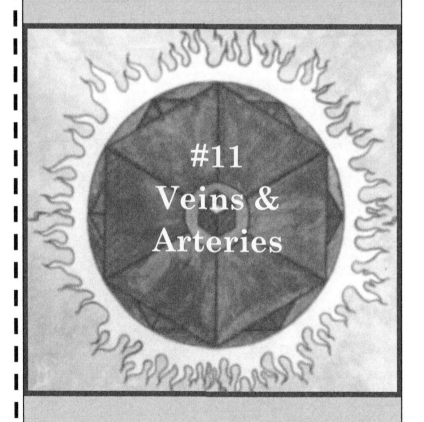

#11
Veins &
Arteries

#11 Veins & Arteries

Action: **Move**

Condition: **Circulation**

Emotion: **Resentment**

Low Emotion: **Gravity**

High Emotion: **Games**

Flashcards for the
SAF Numbering System

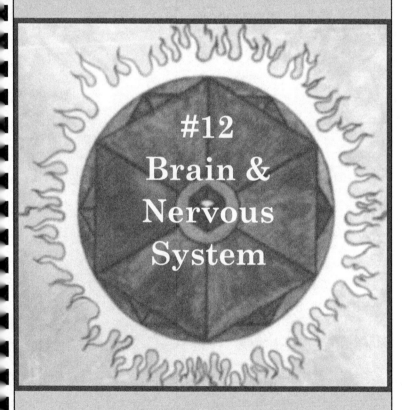

#12
Brain &
Nervous
System

#12 Brain & Nervous System

Action: **Time**

Condition: **Electricity**

Emotion: **Nervous**

Low Emotion: **Complicated**

High Emotion: **Simplify**

Flashcards for the
SAF Numbering System

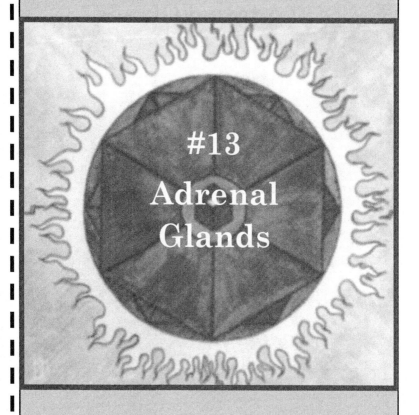

#13
Adrenal
Glands

#13 Adrenal Glands

Action: **Pressure**

Condition: **Capacitance**

Emotion: **Courage**

Low Emotion: **Shame**

High Emotion: **Pride**

Flashcards for the
SAF Numbering System

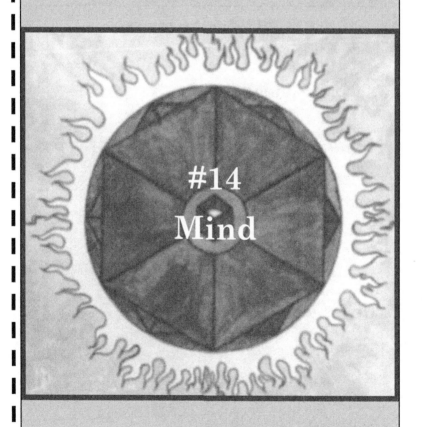

#14
Mind

#14 Mind

Action: **Space**

Condition: **Analyze**

Emotion: **Wonder**

Low Emotion: **Unknown**

High Emotion: **Serenity**

Flashcards for the
SAF Numbering System

#15
Hypothalamus
& the Senses

#15 Hypothalamus & the Senses

Action: **Result**

Condition: **Evaluation**

Emotion: **Attention**

Low Emotion: **Inhibited**

High Emotion: **Communicate**

Flashcards for the
SAF Numbering System

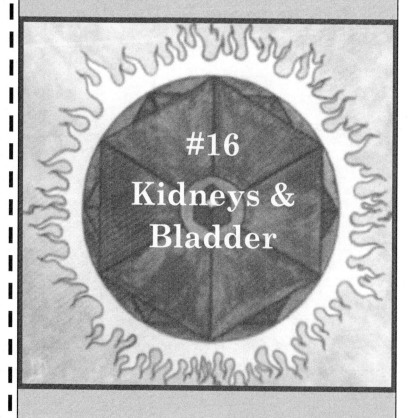

#16
Kidneys &
Bladder

#16 Kidneys & Bladder

Action: **Refuse**

Condition: **Filtration**

Emotion: **Fear**

Low Emotion: **Poisoned**

High Emotion: **Purify**

Flashcards for the
SAF Numbering System

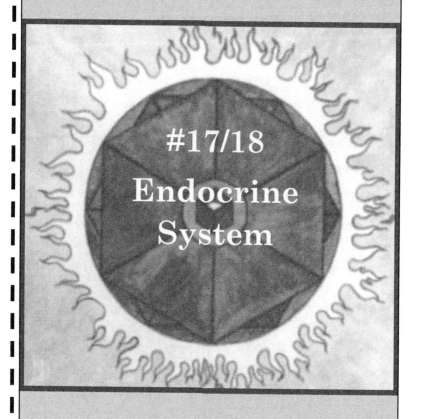

#17/18
Endocrine
System

#17/18 Endocrine System

Action: **Coordinate**

Condition: **Equalize**

Emotion: **Conservative**

Low Emotion: **Perverted**

High Emotion: **Balance**

Flashcards for the
SAF Numbering System

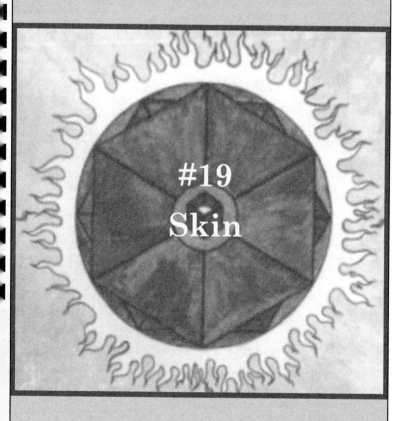

#19
Skin

#19 Skin

Action: **Push**

Condition: **Demarcate**

Emotion: **Boredom**

Low Emotion: **Lost**

High Emotion: **Win**

Flashcards for the
SAF Numbering System

#20
Pancreas &
Solar Plexus

#20 Pancreas & Solar Plexus

Action: **Quality**

Condition: **Location**

Emotion: **Laughter**

Low Emotion: **Suppressed**

High Emotion: **Express**

Flashcards for the
SAF Numbering System

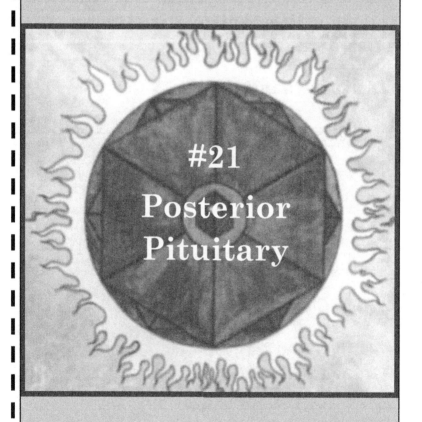

#21
Posterior
Pituitary

#21 Posterior Pituitary

Action: **Quantity**

Condition: **Hydrolyze**

Emotion: **Grief**

Low Emotion: **Stuck**

High Emotion: **Free**

Flashcards for the
SAF Numbering System

#22
Parathyroid

#22 Parathyroid

Action: **Have**

Condition: **Experience**

Emotion: **Anger**

Low Emotion: **Solid**

High Emotion: **Dissect**

Flashcards for the
SAF Numbering System

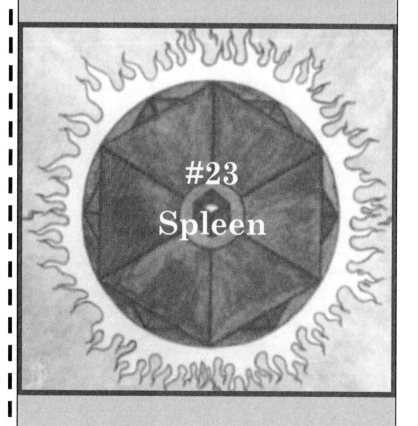

#23
Spleen

#23 Spleen

Action: **Do**

Condition: **Rejection**

Emotion: **Antagonize**

Low Emotion: **Regret**

High Emotion: **Appreciate**

Flashcards for the
SAF Numbering System

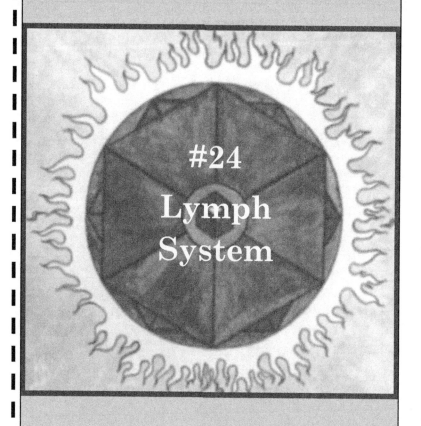

#24
Lymph
System

#24 Lymph System

Action: **Be**

Condition: **Accept**

Emotion: **Enthusiasm**

Low Emotion: **Mystery**

High Emotion: **Understanding**

Index

Printed in Great Britain
by Amazon